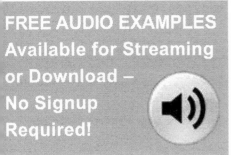

12 EASY CH
FC
12 Classic

MW00883395

By Troy Nelson

ISBN 9798671183757   Copyright © 2020 Troy Nelson Music LLC
International Copyright Secured. All Rights Reserved.

HOW TO GET THE AUDIO

The audio files for this book are available for free as downloads or streaming on *roynelsonmusic.com*.

We are available to help you with your audio downloads and any other questions you may have. Simply email *help@troynelsonmusic.com*.

See below for the recommended ways to listen to the audio:

Download Audio Files (Zipped)	Stream Audio Files
Download Audio Files (Zipped)	• Recommended for CELL PHONES & TABLETS
Recommended for COMPUTERS on WiFi	• Bookmark this page
A ZIP file will automatically download to the default "downloads" folder on your computer	• Simply tap the PLAY button on the track you want to listen to
Recommended: download to a desktop/laptop computer *first*, then transfer to a tablet or cell phone	• Files also available for streaming or download at *soundcloud.com/troynelsonbooks*
Phones & tablets may need an "unzipping" app such as iZip, Unrar or Winzip	
Download on WiFi for faster download speeds	

To download the companion audio files for this book, visit: troynelsonmusic.com/audio-downloads/

INTRODUCTION

I have to confess: I've never learned a Christmas song from beginning to end. I've always intended to. Every year when the leaves begin to change and the wind gets a little colder, I tell myself: "This is the year I'm going to learn a Christmas tune! This is the year I bust out the guitar at mom and dad's house and play 'Jingle Bells' for family and friends! This is the year I dazzle them with my guitar prowess!"

Sadly, it still hasn't happened (yet!). Part of the blame falls on me, obviously, but part of the blame is due to a lack of good resources. As you probably know, learning a Christmas song is no small endeavor; it takes time and dedication. Personally, I'm willing to put in the time, but I always have a problem finding good guitar arrangements. It's not due to a lack of options, because hundreds—if not thousands—of Christmas song arrangements can be found in various books or on countless websites. No, the problem I have is finding arrangements that fit my skill set, sound great, and don't take forever to learn.

Most Christmas songs on the market for guitar players are either highly technical fingerstyle or chord-melody arrangements, or just simple "lead sheets" with melody, lyrics, and chords. Sadly, there's just not much in between, which is where most guitar players reside.

While I'd certainly love to learn an intricate fingerstyle arrangement of "O Come All Ye Faithful," and I did study jazz chord melody in college, the problem is finding enough time to woodshed these types of arrangements. After all, we guitarists are busy people. We have work, family, and other obligations occupying most of our time, so we want something that we can jump into and learn quickly. And that's where *12 Easy Christmas Songs for Solo Guitar* comes in. It fills the void between too easy and too hard.

Each song is arranged in *simple* chord-melody style. If you're unfamiliar, chord melody is simply an arrangement that includes both the melody and the harmony (chords), enabling the guitarist to play solo or in a setting that lacks another melody/harmony instrument, such as a drum/bass/guitar trio. More specifically, the melody and chords are played *at the same time*. The chords generally appear on the same beat of each measure—for example, on beats 1 and 3 in 4/4 time—while the melody is played on top. This means chords are often altered a bit in order to play the melody note on the top string of the chord voicing.

Chord melody is synonymous with jazz, but in lieu of the more sophisticated extended and altered chords of that genre, the arrangements in this book are limited to common open chords. In fact, most songs contain no more than three or four chords. And here's the best part: you need to know just six chords—C, D, Em, F, G, and Am—to play all 12 songs!

In addition to simple chord-melody arrangements, which are notated in easy-to-understand tab, each of the 12 songs contains lyrics and chord diagrams. Therefore, if you're a vocalist who'd rather strum and sing Christmas songs to your friends and family, we've got you covered, too!

The songs in this book might be easy to perform but they sound great and are a lot of fun to play. While absolute beginners may struggle a bit with some of these arrangements, late beginners and intermediate players should be able to pick them up pretty quickly. And sight-reading these songs is certainly not out of the question for advanced guitarists.

READING CHORD DIAGRAMS & TAB

As mentioned in the introduction, the songs in this book are presented in both chord diagrams and in tab. In this section, we're going to go over each format so you'll be able to quickly apply the music to your instrument. Let's start with chord diagrams.

Chord Diagrams

A *chord diagram*, or *chord frame*, is simply a graphical representation of a small section (usually four or five frets) of the guitar neck, or fretboard. Vertical lines represent the guitar's six strings, horizontal lines represent frets, and black dots indicate where your fingers should be placed. Although a bit counterintuitive, chord diagrams are presented as though you're looking at the neck while the guitar is held vertically in front of you, rather than from a more natural horizontal position. Nevertheless, chord frames are a good way to quickly understand how a chord should be "voiced," or fingered.

A thick, black horizontal line at the top of the diagram indicates the guitar's nut (the plastic-like string-spacer at the end of the fretboard). When this is present, the chord typically incorporates one or more open strings, which are represented by hollow circles above the frame. Conversely, when an open string is not to be played, an "X" will appear above the frame.

When more than one note is fretted by the same finger, or "barred," a slur encompasses the notes, which can range from two to six strings (*barre chords* get their name from this technique). If a chord is played higher up the neck, above the 4th or 5th fret, the nut is replaced by a thin horizontal line and the fret number is indicated next to the lowest fret (highest in the diagram). Sometimes—but not always—the chord's fingering is included at the bottom of the frame: 1 = index, 2 = middle, 3 = ring, 4 = pinky, and T = thumb.

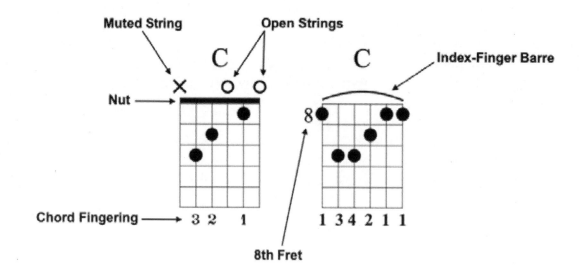

6

Tab

As a form of music notation, tab has been around for centuries. However, it has really exploded in popularity among guitar players the past few decades, particularly since the advent of the Internet. The reason for its popularity is the simple fact that it's so easy to learn and use.

A tab staff looks much like a standard treble clef; however, if you look a little closer, you'll notice that it contains *six* lines instead of five. Those six lines represent the six strings of the guitar, with the low E string positioned at the bottom, and the high E string at the top. Tab contains no key signature because note-reading is not involved; instead, numbers are placed on the strings to represent the frets of the guitar neck. For example, if you see the number 3 on the low E (6th) string, you would press down on fret 3 of that string. Or, if you see the number 0 stacked on the D and G (4th and 3rd) strings, you would pluck those two strings together, open (unfretted).

Sometimes, you'll see tab accompanied by standard notation, and other times, you'll see tab-only music. Like standard notation, tab-only music often includes rhythms (stems, flags, beams, rests, etc.). Rhythm symbols in tab are the same as the ones you'll find in standard notation, only the noteheads are replaced by fret numbers.

Regardless of what type of tab is used, a time signature will be present. The *time signature* is a pair of numbers stacked on top of each other at the beginning of a piece of music (immediately after the key signature in standard notation). The top number indicates how many beats comprise each *measure*, or *bar* (the space between the vertical *bar lines*), while the bottom number indicates which note is equivalent to one beat (2 = half note, 4 = quarter note, 8 = eighth note, etc.). Seven of the songs in this book are played in 4/4 time, meaning each measure contains four beats (upper number), and quarter notes are equivalent to one beat (bottom number), while the other five songs are played in 3/4 time, and each measure contains three beats.

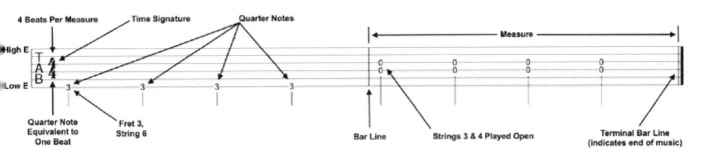

7

THE CHORDS

As mentioned in the introduction, six chords are all the stand between you and the 12 songs in this book. The voicings for each song are illustrated above the tab staffs, but let's preview the chords here in case some of them are new to you.

The six chords below serve two purposes: 1) they're the voicings you'll strum if you plan to strum and sing the songs, and 2) they provide the framework for the chords used in the chord-melody arrangements. If you're unfamiliar with any of these chords, get to know them now. That way, you'll be ready to jump in and learn any one of the 12 songs.

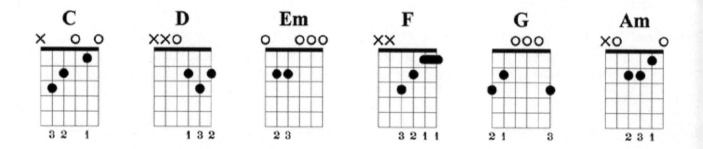

As you start to learn the chord melodies, you'll quickly discover that alternative voicings and fingerings must be employed. Below are seven voicings that are either entirely new chord types (Cadd9, D7, G7, and Gmaj7) or are alternate fingerings for some of the chords above (C, Em, and G). Despite these new chord types/fingerings, the six chords above are still the fundamental chords of the arrangements. Get to know these alternate chords, as well, as they will come in handy very soon.

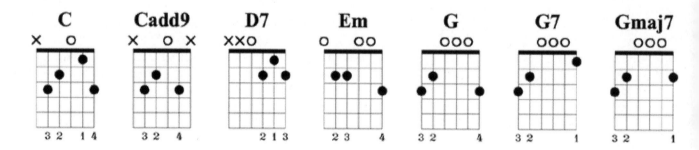

HOW TO CHANGE KEYS

All 12 songs in this book are either arranged in the key of C or the key of G. However, if you prefer to play any of them in a different key, all you need is a capo. If you're unfamiliar, a *capo* is a device that clamps onto the guitar's neck to shorten the length of the strings, thereby transposing the music to another key, which is determined by the fret on which the capo is placed.

The following diagrams will help with changing keys. The first diagram illustrates the various keys on the neck when using the open C chord as the tonic (root) chord. For example, to play in the key of C# simply place the capo on fret 1 and strum the C chord (index finger should now be on fret 2). To play in the key of D, just slide the capo up to fret 2 (and voice the C chord at fret 3).

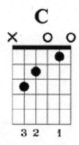

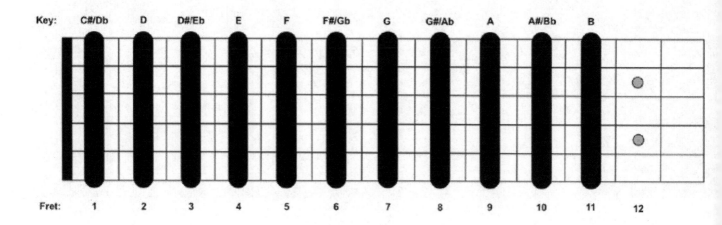

The same principle applies to the open G chord. For example, to play in the key of A, place the capo at fret 2 and strum the G chord (now voiced with the middle finger on fret 5 of string 6). To play in the key of B, simply slide the capo up to fret 4 and strum the G chord (now voiced on fret 7).

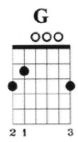

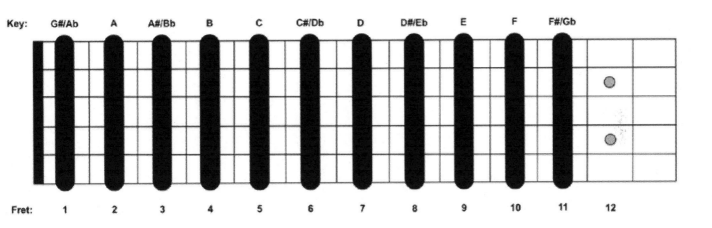

When using a capo while playing the chord melodies, it's important to remember that the tab numbers are relative to the capoed fret. In other words, the capoed fret acts as the nut, so when you see a "0" (zero) in tab, you should still play the string "open," but now it rings at a higher pitch due to the capo's position on the neck. The other tab numbers are relative to the capo as well, so when you see a "1" on, say, the low E string, you should voice that string on the fret directly adjacent to the capo. For example, if the capo is placed on fret 5, you would voice that note on fret 6, which is fret 1 ("1") in tab. In other words, just envision the capoed fret as the open strings ("0" in tab) and play all other notes accordingly.

ANGELS WE HAVE HEARD ON HIGH

KEY: C

TIP: For the chord melody, you'll want to use the alternate fingering for the G chord—the one shown in the introduction with the ring finger on string 6, middle on string 5, and pinky on string 1. This will help you play the melody notes on top, particularly when moving from G (fret 3, string 1) to F (fret 1, string 1)

WATCH OUT FOR: The first bar of the chorus. Here, you'll play an open C chord but with the pinky voicing the high G note (fret 3, string 1). Then, while keeping the pinky in place, you'll slide from fret 3 to fret 5 and then back down to fret 3 for the pull-offs.

STRUM PATTERN:

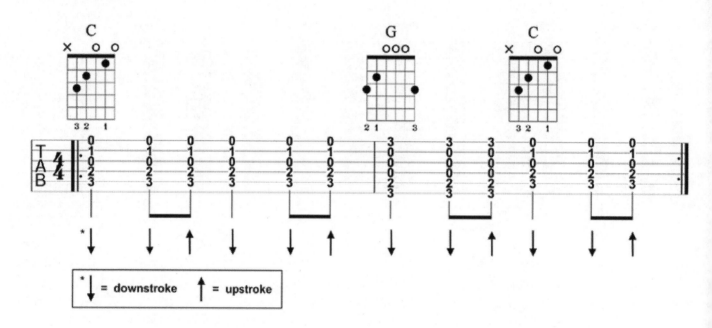

Chord Melody **Strumming**

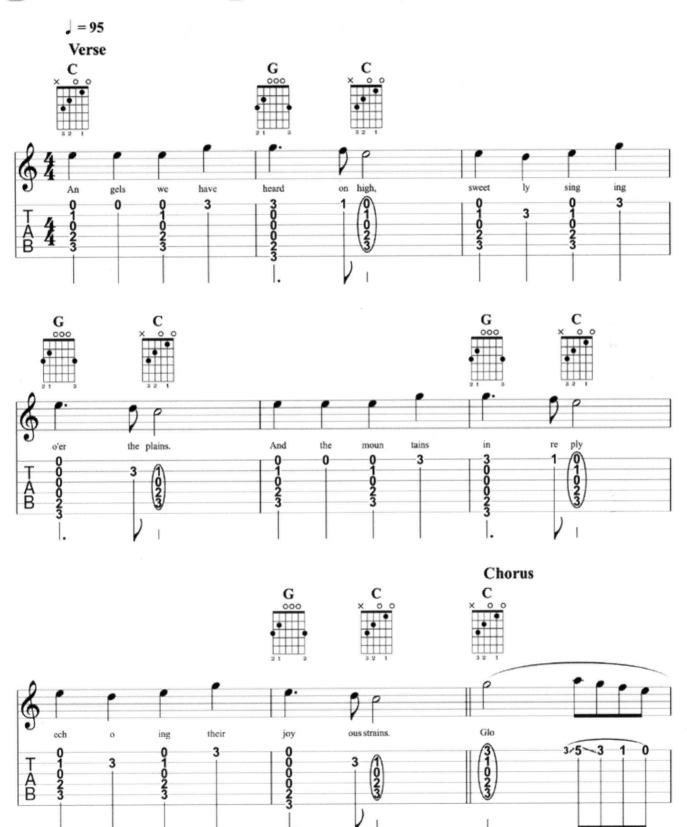

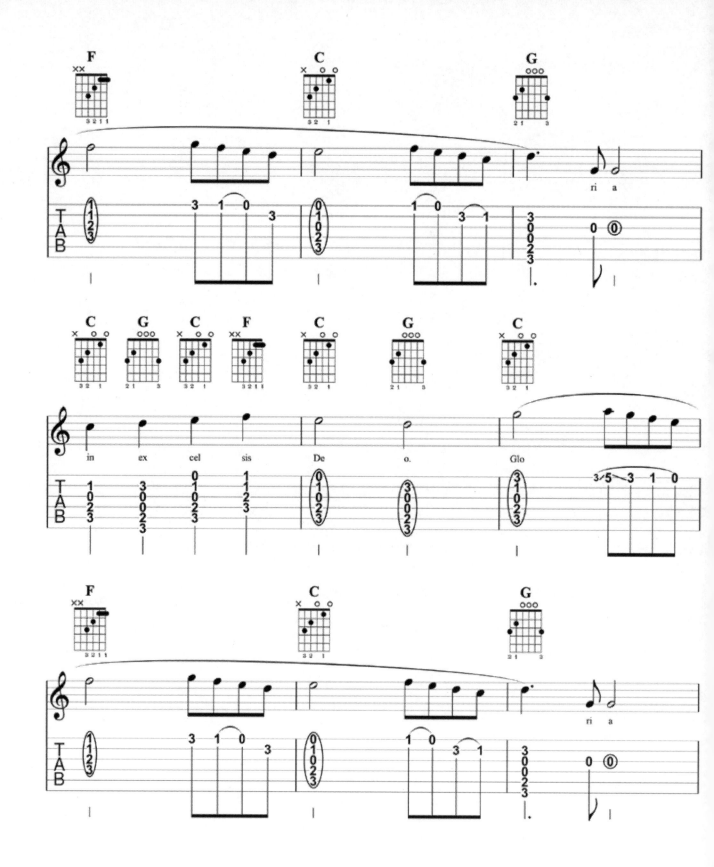

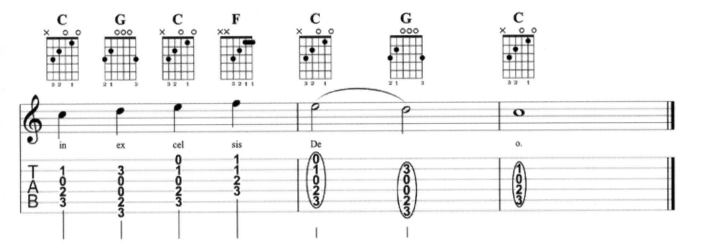

Additional Lyrics

2. Shepherds, why this jubilee?
   Why your joyous strains prolong?
   What the gladsome tidings be
   Which inspire your heavenly song?
   Gloria in excelsis Deo
   Gloria in excelsis Deo

3. Come to Bethlehem and see
   Him whose birth the angles sing
   Come adore on bended knee
   Christ the Lord, the newborn King
   Gloria in excelsis Deo
   Gloria in excelsis Deo

AULD LANG SYNE

KEY: G

TIP: In bar 1, voice the G chord as indicated in the chord frame above the staff, using your pinky to grab the F♯ note that falls on the "and" of beat 2. Be sure to keep your fingers in place for the G chord as you do this, however, so you'll be ready to rearticulate the chord on beat 3.

WATCH OUT FOR: The Em–C chord change. Although neither chord is overly difficult to voice, the challenge here is playing the E note (fret 2, string 4) on the "and" of beat 2 and then immediately having to play the two-note C chord on beat 3. The best strategy here is to make the chord change a half beat early; in other words, play the E note with whatever finger you plan to use for the C chord voicing.

STRUM PATTERN:

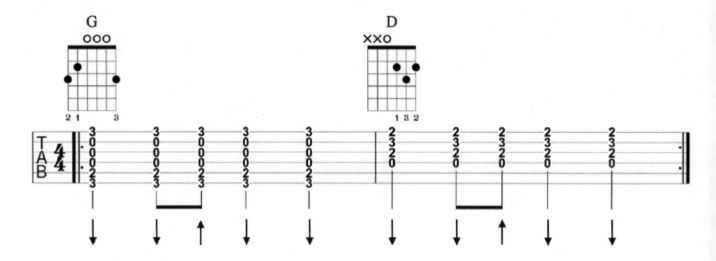

 **Chord Melody**  **Strumming**

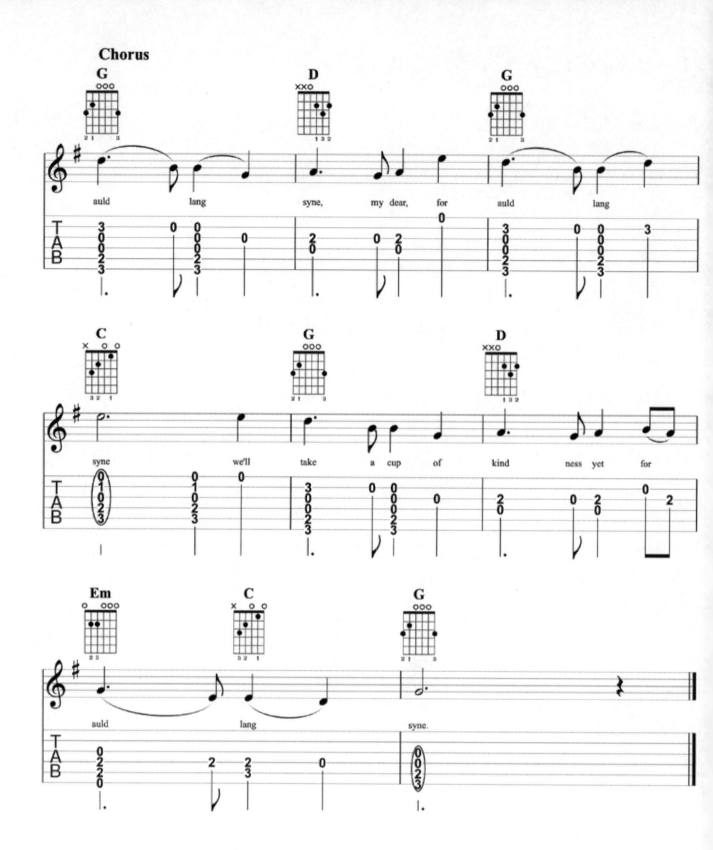

AWAY IN A MANGER

KEY: C

TIP: In bar 5, use the alternate voicing of the G chord so your ring finger is on fret 3 of string 6 and your middle finger on fret 2 of string 5. That way, you can use your index finger to voice the A note (fret 2, string 3) while leaving the other fingers in place and allowing the G chord to ring throughout the measure.

WATCH OUT FOR: The fourth measure from the end. Although the chord diagram above the staff is a standard G chord, you'll need to use the G7 chord voicing from the introduction to start this measure because the melody note on top (string 1) is F, which happens to be the 7th (minor 7th, to be precise) of the G7 chord.

STRUM PATTERN:

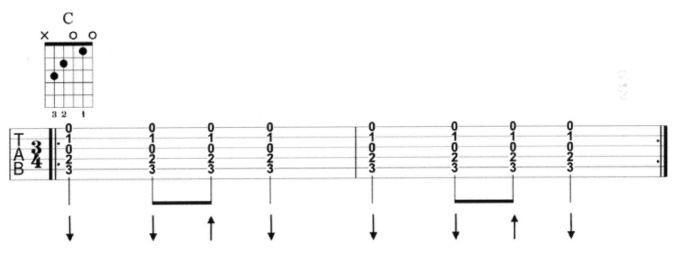

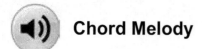 **Chord Melody**  **Strumming**

Away in a manger, no crib for a bed. The little Lord Jesus laid down His sweet head The stars in the sky looked down where He

20

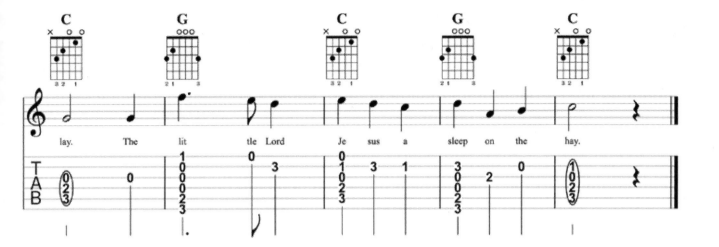

Additional Lyrics

2. The Cattle are lowing, the baby awakes
   But little Lord Jesus no crying he makes
   I love Thee, Lord Jesus; look down from the sky
   And stay by my cradle 'til morning is nigh

3. Be near me, Lord Jesus; I ask Thee to stay
   Close by me forever and love me, I pray
   Bless all the dear children in thy tender care
   And take us to heaven, to live with Thee there

THE FIRST NOEL

KEY: G

TIP: You'll want to use the alternate voicings for both the C chord and the G chord because a lot of index-finger melody playing is required. The same goes for the Em chord in measure 5, where you'll play the high G (fret 3) and F♯ (fret 2) notes on string 1 with your pinky.

WATCH OUT FOR: The melody notes in measure 7. This one looks easy at first glance, but the challenge here is shifting your pinky from string 1 to string 2 at the same fret (fret 3) while allowing the lower portion of the C chord (strings 3–5) to ring throughout the measure.

STRUM PATTERN:

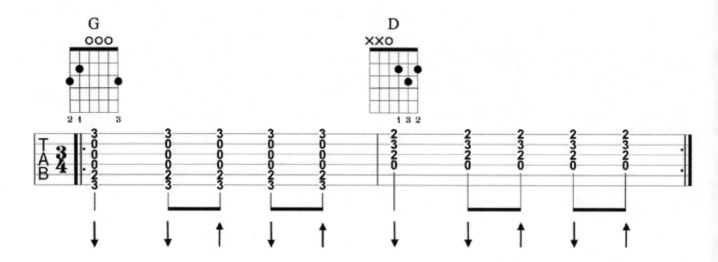

 **Chord Melody**   **Strumming**

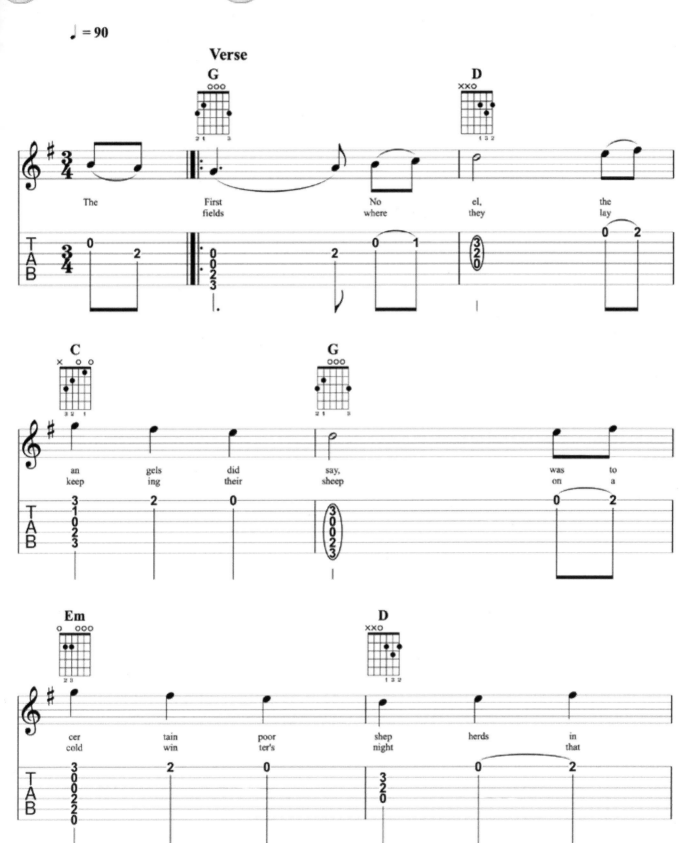

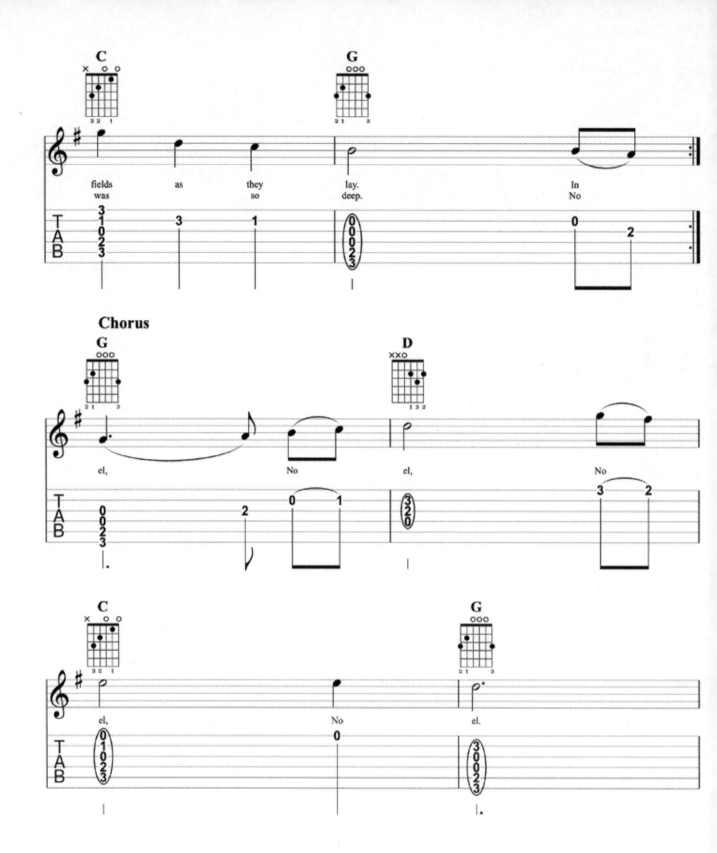

Chorus

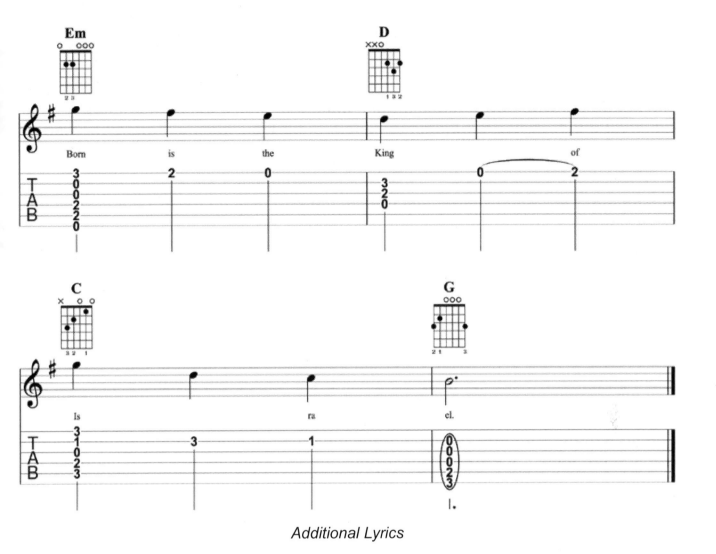

Additional Lyrics

2. They looked up and saw a star
   Shining in the East beyond them far
   And to the earth it gave great light
   And so it continued both day and night
   Noel, Noel, Noel, Noel
   Born is the King of Israel

3. And by the light of the same star
   Three wisemen came from country far
   To seek for a King was their intent
   And to follow the star wherever it went
   Noel, Noel, Noel, Noel
   Born is the King of Israel

4. This star drew nigh to the Northwest
   O'er Bethlehem it took its rest
   And there it did both pause and stay
   Right o'er the place where Jesus lay
   Noel, Noel, Noel, Noel
   Born is the King of Israel

5. Then entered in those wisemen three
   Full reverently upon their knee
   And offered there in His Presence
   Their gold and myrrh and frankincense
   Noel, Noel, Noel, Noel
   Born is the King of Israel

6. Then let us all with one accord
   Sing praise to our heavenly Lord
   That hath made Heaven and earth of nought
   And with his blood mankind hath bought
   Noel, Noel, Noel, Noel
   Born is the King of Israel

HARK! THE HERALD ANGELS SING

KEY: G

TIP: In measures 15 and 19, use the D7 chord voicing that was presented in the introduction. Even though the top string is never played, the D7 chord will put your index finger in an advantageous position to perform the second-string hammer-ons.

WATCH OUT FOR: The trio of single notes that bridge measures 7 and 8. While voicing these notes is a breeze, the hard part is playing them in time, because it's very easy to rush this section. Therefore, be sure to use a metronome or rhythm track as you practice this song—and all the other songs, as well. Also, be sure to listen to the audio demonstration to hear how it should sound when played in time.

STRUM PATTERN:

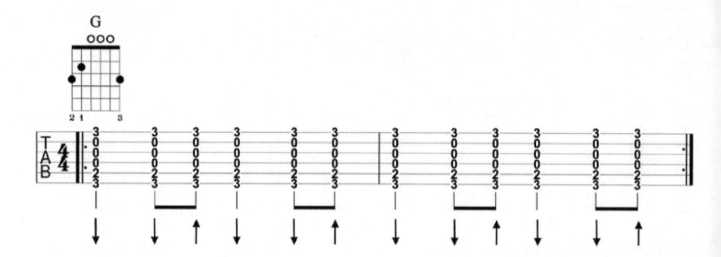

Chord Melody  **Strumming**

27

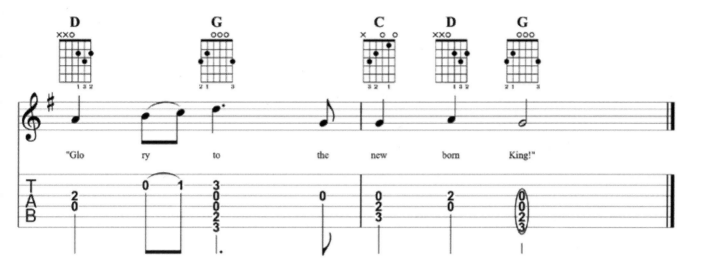

"Glo ry to the new born King!"

Additional Lyrics

. Christ by highest heaven adored
Christ, the everlasting Lord
Late in time behold Him come
Offspring of the Virgin's womb
Veiled in flesh the Godhead see
Hail the incarnate Deity
Pleased as man with man to dwell
Jesus, our Emmanuel
Hark! The herald angels sing,
"Glory to the newborn King!"

3. Hail the Heaven-born Prince of Peace!
Hail the Son of Righteousness!
Light and life to all He brings
Raised with healing in His wings
He lays His glory by
Born that man no more may die
Born to raise the sons of earth
Born to give them second birth
Hark! The herald angels sing,
"Glory to the newborn King!"

JINGLE BELLS

KEY: C

TIP: In measures 5–6 and 13–14 of the chorus, keep your index finger barred across strings 1–2 as you shift your middle and ring fingers to change from the F chord to the C chord. That way, the index finger will be in position to play the F melody note (fret 1, string 1) on beat 1 of the C-chord measure and no extraneous finger-shifting will be required.

WATCH OUT FOR: The high A note (fret 5, string 1) in measure 15 of the verse. You'll want to voice this note, as well as the G note (fret 3) that follows, with your pinky, which will put your other fingers in an advantageous position for the subsequent G7 chord (beat 3). In fact, you'll want to use the alternate voicing for the G chord (shown in the introduction) in measure 14, as well, and use your pinky for all of the notes along string 1 that precede the G7 chord.

STRUM PATTERN:

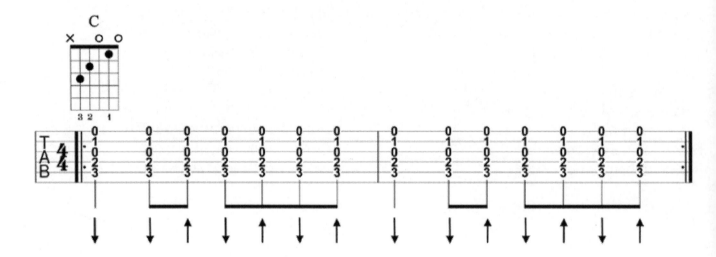

Chord Melody **Strumming**

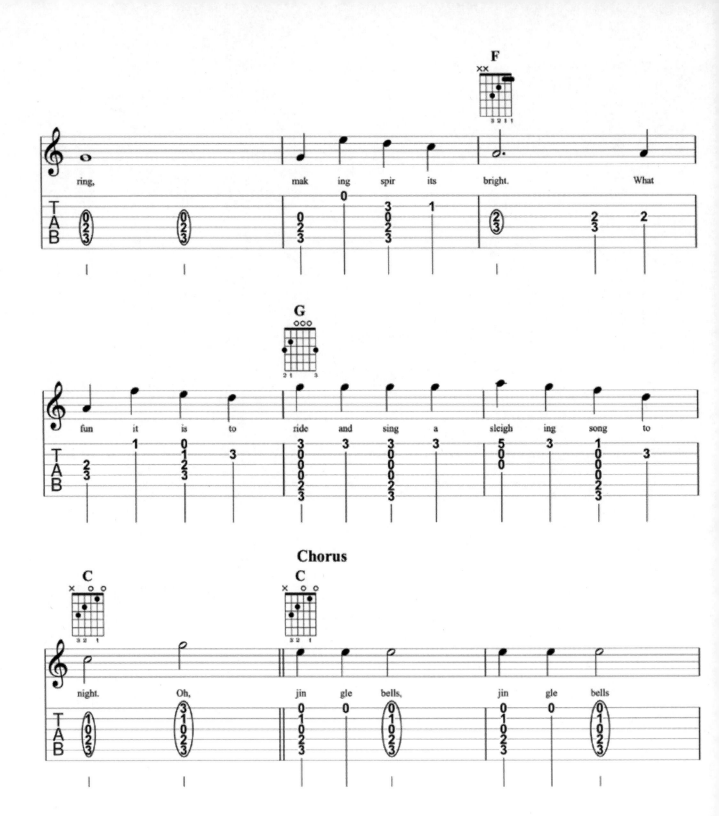

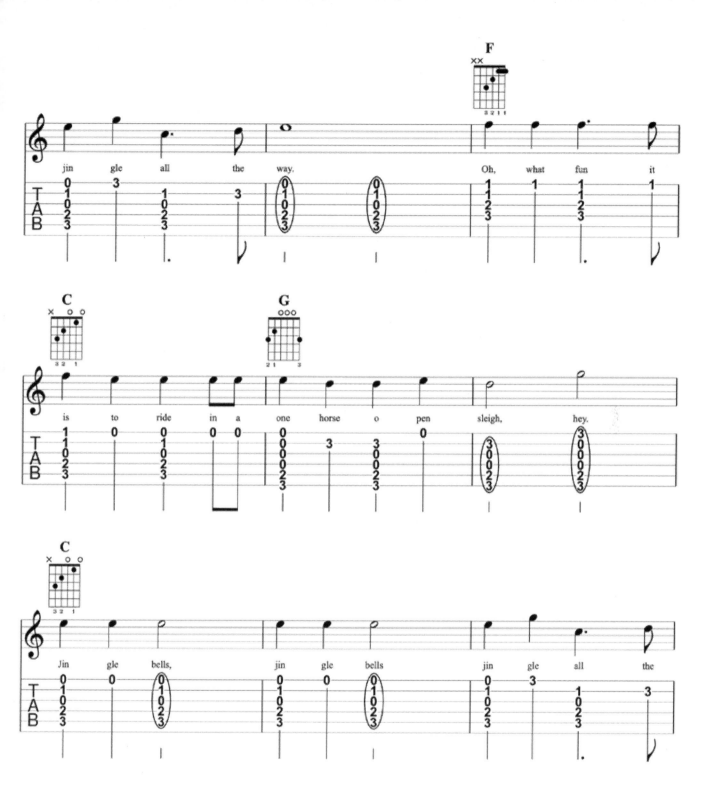

Additional Lyrics

2. A day or two ago
   I thought I'd take a ride
   And soon Miss Fanny Bright
   Was seated by my side
   The horse was lean and lank
   Misfortune seemed his lot
   He got into a drifted bank
   And then we got upsot

4. Now the ground is white
   Go it while you're young
   Take the girls tonight
   And sing this sleighing song
   Just get a bobtailed bay
   Two forty as his speed
   Hitch him to an open sleigh
   And crack, you'll take the lead

3. A day or two ago
   The story I must tell
   I went out on the snow
   And on my back I fell
   A gent was riding by
   In a one-horse open sleigh
   He laughed as there I sprawling lie
   But quickly drove away

JOY TO THE WORLD

KEY: G

TIP: In measure 1, use the G (alternate) and Gmaj7 chord voicings that were presented in the intro-duction, which will make chord-switching more efficient. A similar strategy should also be employed in measures 9 and 11. This will allow the lower portion of the chord to ring as you switch melody notes from G to F♯.

WATCH OUT FOR: The 8th notes on beat 1 of measures 13 and 15. It's easy to rush this rhythm, so be sure to play along with a metronome or rhythm track. For best results, use alternate (down–up) picking for these two notes.

STRUM PATTERN:

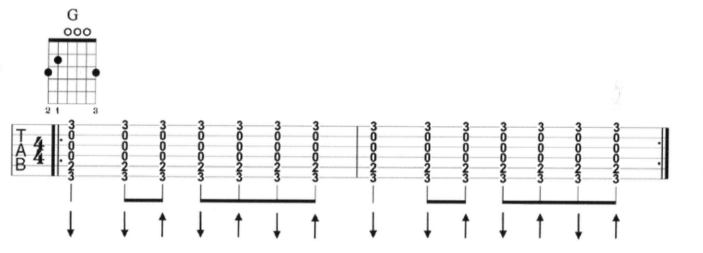

 **Chord Melody** **Strumming**

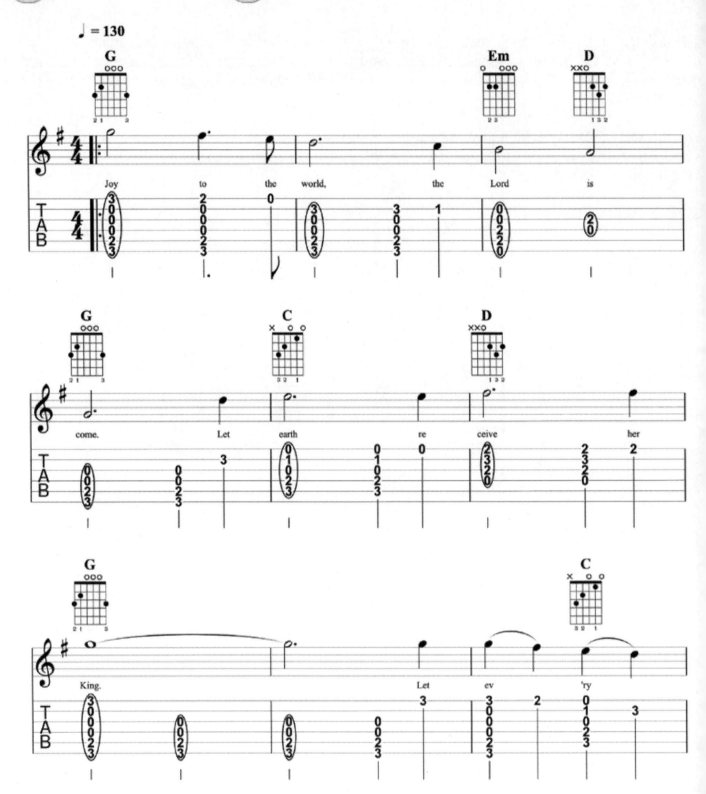

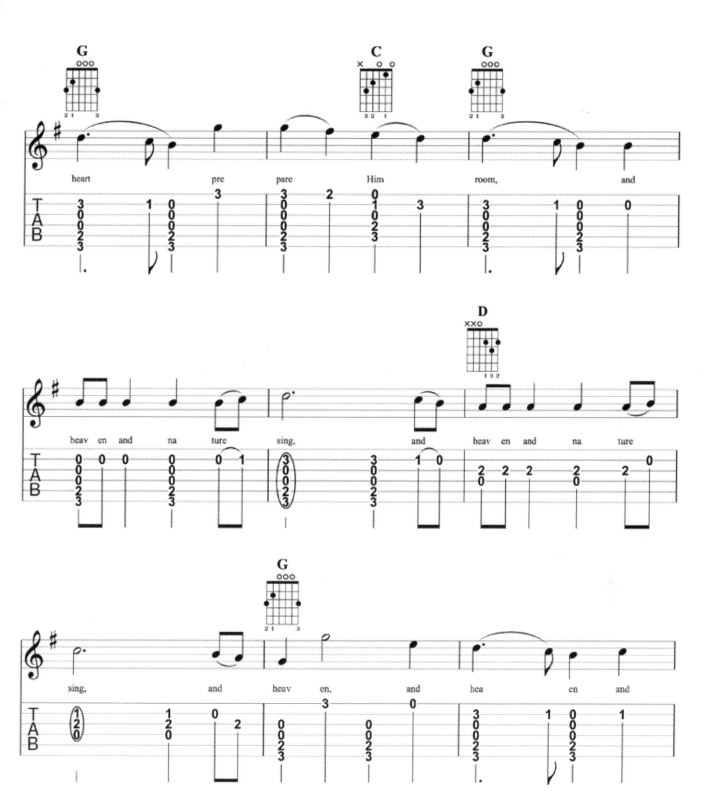

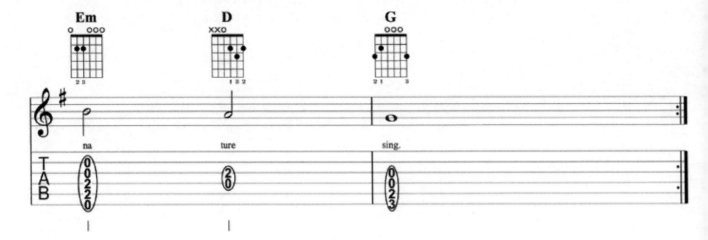

Additional Lyrics

2. Joy to the world, the Savior reigns
   Let men their songs employ
   While fields and floods, rocks, hills, and plains
   Repeat the sounding joy,
   Repeat the sounding joy,
   Repeat, repeat the sounding joy

4. He rules the world with truth and grace
   And makes the nations prove
   The glories of His righteousness
   And wonders of His love,
   And wonders of His love
   And wonders, and wonders of His love

3. No more let sins and sorrows grow
   Nor thorns infest the ground
   He comes to make His blessings flow
   Far as the curse is found,
   Far as the curse is found,
   Far as, far as the curse is found

O CHRISTMAS TREE

KEY: G

TIP: This is the only time in this book that you'll encounter the rhythmic combination of a dotted 8th and 16th note. Therefore, I suggest listening to the audio demonstration if you find yourself struggling with the rhythm.

WATCH OUT FOR: Measures where the D chord is played. Since most of these bars contain the note C (fret 1, string 2) in the melody, the D7 voicing that was presented in the introduction will need to be employed (even though the top string is never used).

STRUM PATTERN:

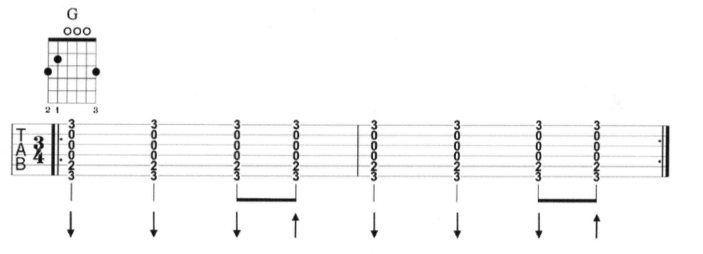

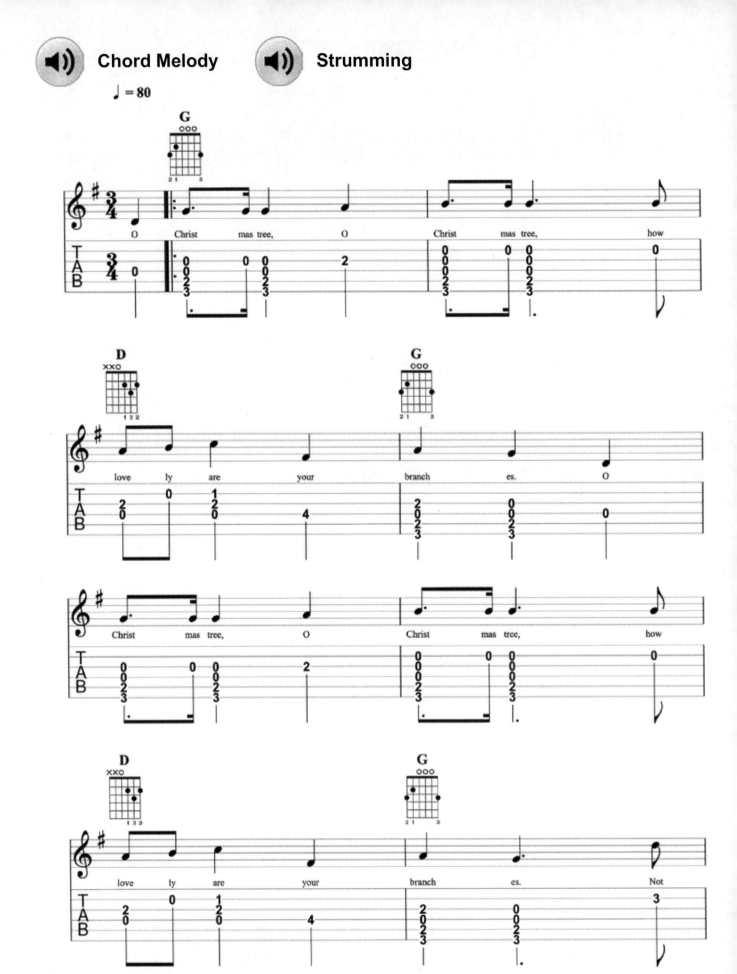

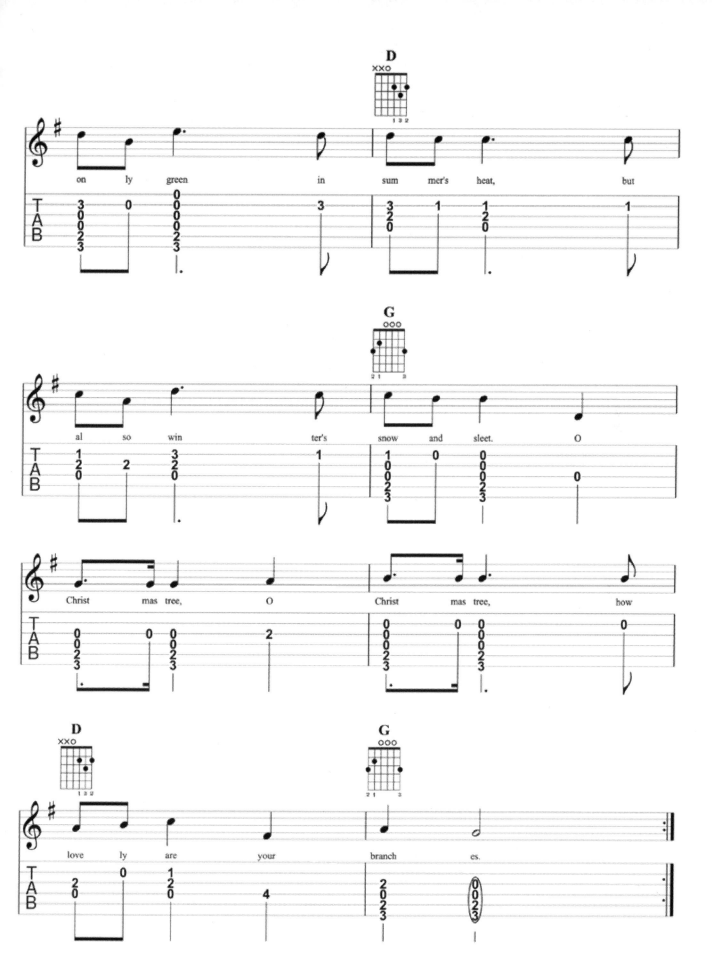

2. O Christmas tree, O Christmas tree,
   Of all the trees most lovely
   O Christmas tree, O Christmas tree,
   Of all the trees most lovely
   Each year you bring to us delight
   With brightly shining Christmas light
   O Christmas tree, O Christmas tree,
   Of all the trees most lovely

3. O Christmas tree, O Christmas tree,
   We learn from all your beauty
   O Christmas tree, O Christmas tree,
   We learn from all your beauty
   Your bright green leaves with festive cheer
   Give hope and strength throughout the year
   O Christmas tree, O Christmas tree,
   We learn from all your beauty

O COME ALL YE FAITHFUL

KEY: C

TIP: For the F chord in measures 3 and 9 of the verse, as well as measure 5 of the chorus, keep your ring, middle, and index fingers affixed to strings 4, 3, and 2, respectively, while you roll your index finger onto and off of string 1 to alternate between the E (open) and F (fret 1) melody notes. To do this, bring your elbow towards your midsection to barre the top two strings, and move it away for your midsection to release the barre. This will help to change the arch of your fretting fingers.

WATCH OUT FOR: Bar 10 of the verse. Although the diagram above the staff indicates a regular G chord, the melody note on beats 1–2 is an F, so you'll need to play the G7 chord that was presented in the introduction, which features F on the top string.

STRUM PATTERN:

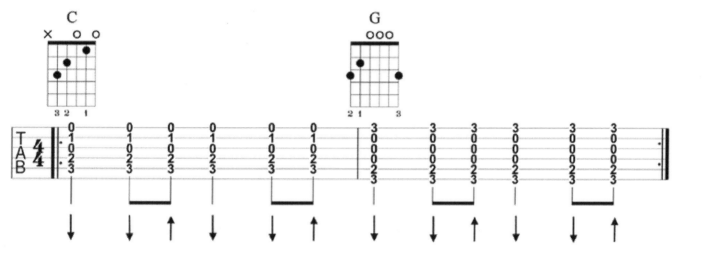

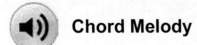 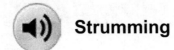

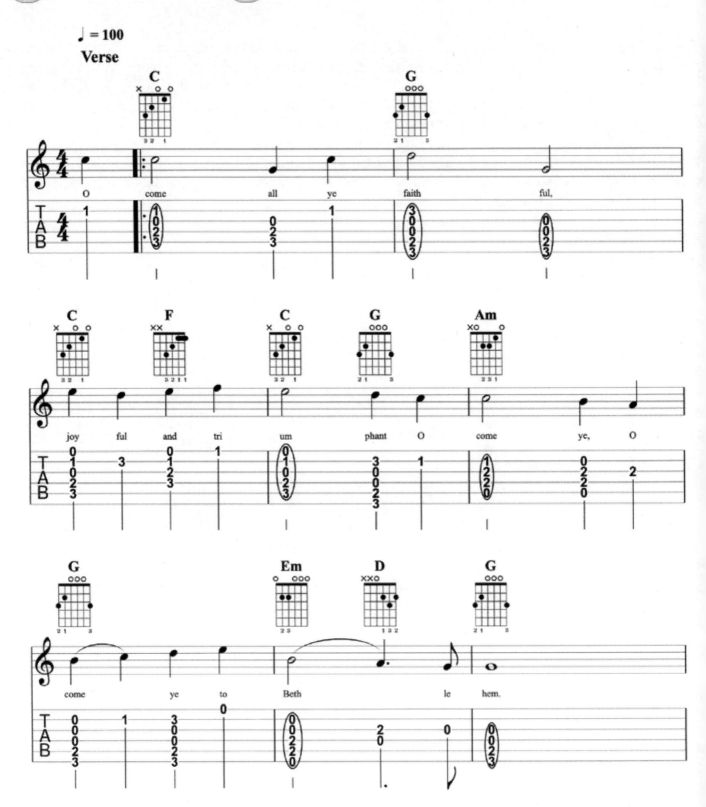

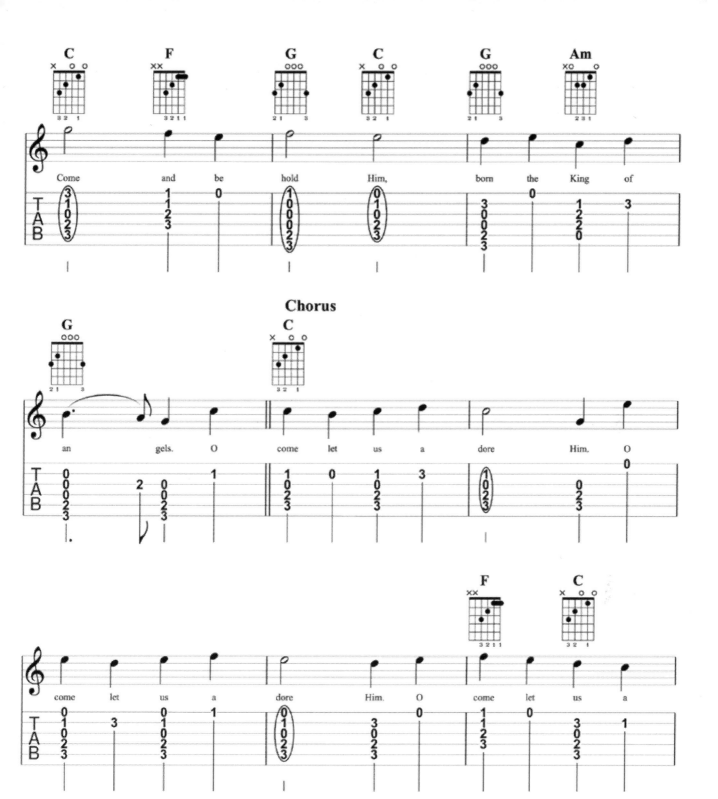

45

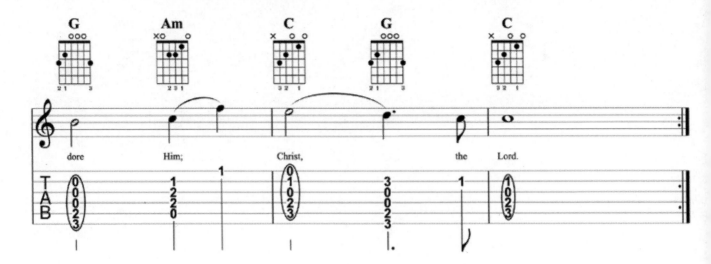

dore   Him;   Christ,   the   Lord.

Additional Lyrics

2. Sing, choirs of angels, sing in exultation
   Sing, all ye citizens of heaven above
   Glory to God, Glory in the highest
   O come let us adore him,
   O come let us adore him,
   O come let us adore him;
   Christ, the Lord

3. Yea, Lord, we greet thee,
   Born this happy morning
   Jesus, to Thee be all glory given
   Son of the Father, now in flesh appearing
   O come let us adore him,
   O come let us adore him,
   O come let us adore him;
   Christ, the Lord

SILENT NIGHT

KEY: C

TIP: In measures 1, 3, 11, and 15, use your index finger to play the A (fret 2, string 3) melody notes. That way, you can keep the lower portion of the C chord fretted, allowing it to ring throughout the measure.

WATCH OUT FOR: The G7 chord in bar 18. This voicing was presented in the introduction and is needed here to play the F melody note on the top string. For the sake of finger efficiency, try playing the preceding measure with the alternate version of the G chord—the one with the ring finger on string 6—which will set up your fret hand nicely for the G7 chord.

STRUM PATTERN:

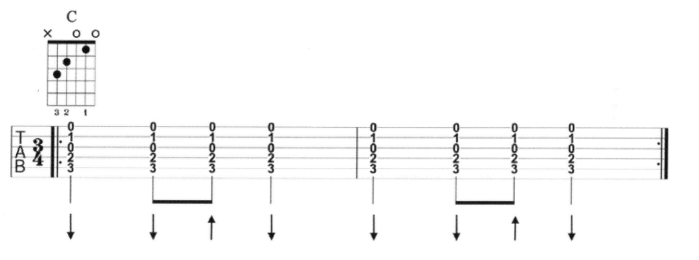

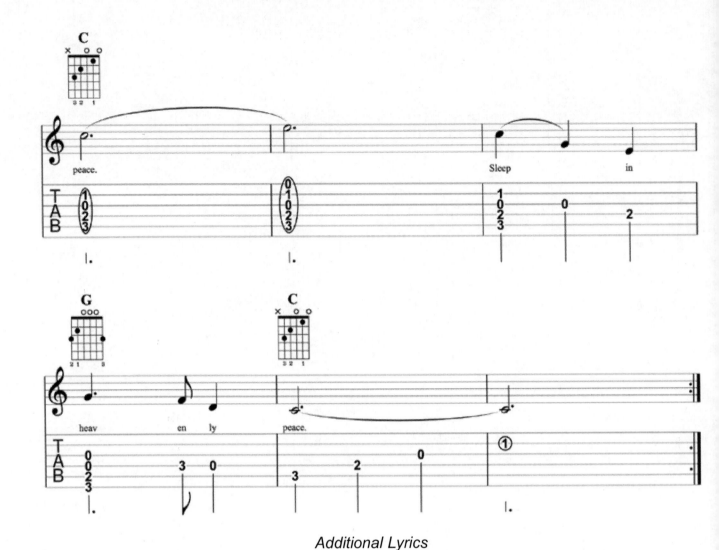

Additional Lyrics

2. Silent night, holy night
   Shepherds quake at the sight
   Glories stream from heaven afar
   Heavenly hosts sing 'Alleluia
   Christ, the Savior, is born
   Christ, the Savior, is born

3. Silent night, holy night
   Son of God, love's pure light
   Radiant beams from Thy holy face
   With the dawn of redeeming grace
   Jesus, Lord, at Thy birth
   Jesus, Lord, at Thy birth

UP ON THE HOUSETOP

KEY: G

TIP: Use a down–up picking combo for all of the 8th-note rhythms. For example, in measure 1, strum the G chord on beat 1 with a downstroke, then use a down–up combo for the two single notes on beat 2.

WATCH OUT FOR: The D chord in bar 3 of the chorus. Although the chord frame above the staff is a common open D chord, the melody note on beats 3–4 is a C, which is not found in that chord. Therefore, you'll need to employ the D7 chord voicing that was presented in the introduction, leaving out the top string, which is not needed in this particular case.

STRUM PATTERN:

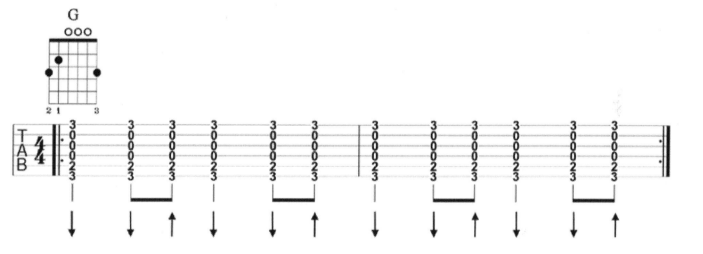

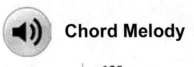 **Chord Melody** **Strumming**

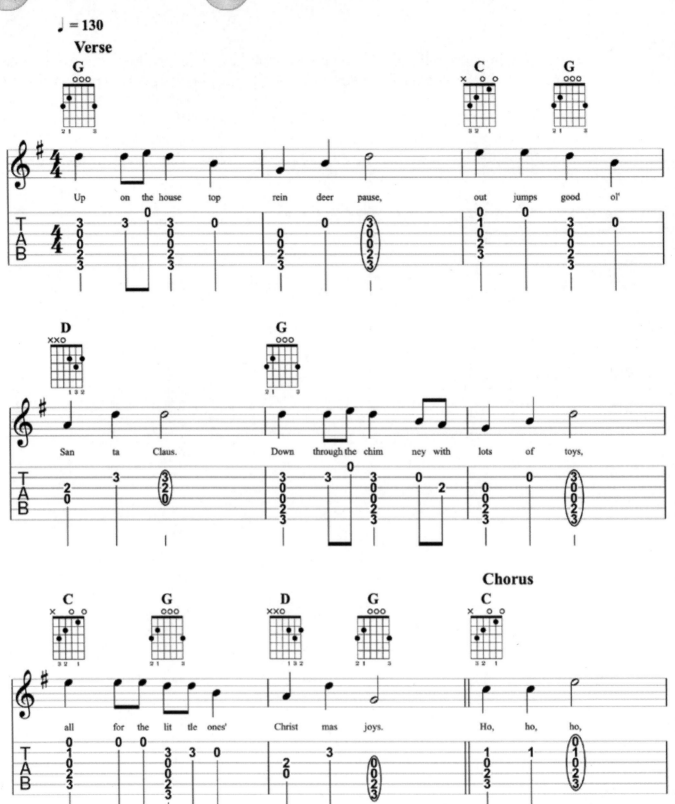

52

Additional Lyrics

2. First comes the stocking of little Nell
   Oh, dear Santa, fill it well
   Give her a dolly that laughs and cries,
   One that will open and shut her eyes
   Ho, ho, ho, who wouldn't go?
   Ho, ho, ho, who wouldn't go?
   Up on the housetop, click, click, click
   Down through the chimney with good Saint Nick

3. Next comes the stocking of little Will
   Oh, just see what a glorious fill
   Here is a hammer and lots of tacks,
   Whistle and ball and a whip that cracks
   Ho, ho, ho, who wouldn't go?
   Ho, ho, ho, who wouldn't go?
   Up on the housetop, click, click, click
   Down through the chimney with good Saint Nick

WE WISH YOU A MERRY CHRISTMAS

KEY: C

TIP: At the end of measure 3, use your ring and index fingers to perform the pull-off. Then, for the subsequent G chord, use the alternate voicing presented in the introduction—the one with the ring finger on string 6. This is the most efficient voicing for getting into the chord, as well as for switching to the C chord in the following measure.

WATCH OUT FOR: The F chord in measures 6 and 11. You'll be inclined to release the chord in order to play the single notes that follow in each measure, but the best strategy is to keep the chord voiced throughout the measure, only releasing certain fingers out of necessity (i.e., to articulate other melody notes).

STRUM PATTERN:

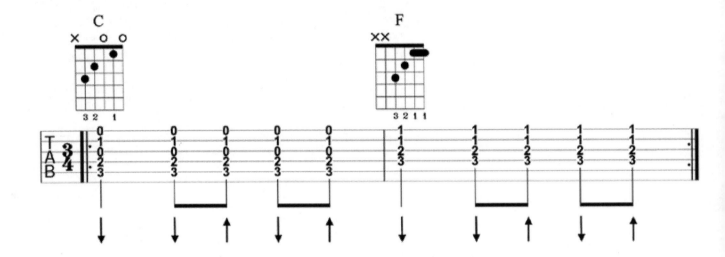

Chord Melody   **Strumming**

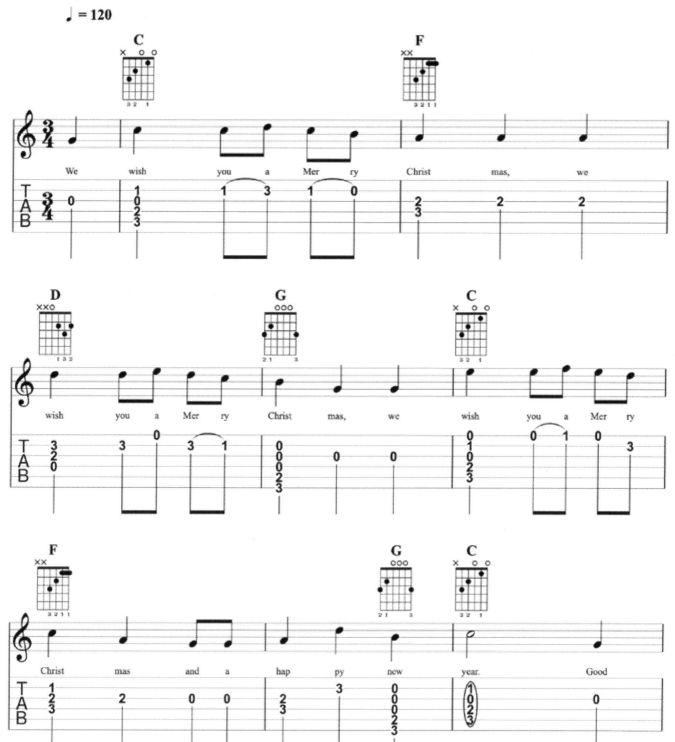

2. Oh, bring us some figgy pudding
   Oh, bring us some figgy pudding
   Oh, bring us some figgy pudding
   And bring it right here
   Good tidings we bring
   To you and your kin
   We wish you a Merry Christmas
   And a happy new year

4. We all like our figgy pudding
   We all like our figgy pudding
   We all like our figgy pudding
   With all its good cheer
   Good tidings we bring
   To you and your kin
   We wish you a Merry Christmas
   And a happy new year

3. We won't go until we get some
   We won't go until we get some
   We won't go until we get some
   So, bring it right here
   Good tidings we bring
   To you and your kin
   We wish you a Merry Christmas
   And a happy new year

5. We wish you a Merry Christmas
   We wish you a Merry Christmas
   We wish you a Merry Christmas
   And a happy new year

Made in United States
Troutdale, OR
11/08/2024

24559362R00033